Perseverance Of The Human Spirit

By Esha Montgomery

Copyright

Perseverance Of The Human Spirit
© 2020 Esha Montgomery

Table Of Contents

Contents

Dedication

A great many things have occurred since the creation of this book began. I have discovered a great reservoir of hope and happiness. It is created by the love and recognition of family, friends and supporters. As a creative my need for input and kind words is unlimited and it takes patience, positive gestures and encouragement in order to make progress. No one can make strides and succeed at them alone. So I would like to thank my Mother, Father, Sister and Craig for showing me patience by reading my work and nurturing my artistic exploration. Much like a daisy; it grows fuller and fuller by the day. This book is a thank you message for the people and the readers in my life who support me on a daily basis.

Prologue

Do your thing! Live, love, travel, pray, hope and never give up in your dreams. So often we chase after the goals that are easy to achieve and ignore our desires that require more effort...Today, I am fighting like never before to turn my fantasies into reality and I hope this book pushes you to do the same. Perseverance of The Human Spirit is centered on the strength and acceptance I have found from readers, family and friends to persevere in my writing journey. Thank you for your ongoing support and well wishes.

Oasis

a single blade of grass
has little significance in a prairie
but it means everything
in a barren land
it draws you to the oasis
hidden in the sand
-Esha

Part 1

Keep Going

Roll your shoulders back
Lift your face to the sky
Love lives within you
Anyone with a brain
Can give up
But only the courageous
That possesses a stout heart
Will keep fighting
With the desire to win

We Are

we are not monolithic
we speak different tongues
come from many lands
come in many colors

spread over space and time
we were here
when civilization began
with night on our back

and a flame in our hand
the first woman to give birth to man
some call us...
the dawn keepers

Artisans

through the windows
of the nonprofit agency
i see… brown dismal trees,
the leaves ate off by winter breeze

the freeze ate up the green
turned it inside out
the blue dragon blowing air
out an unforgiving mouth

i am a poet,
a member of the collective…
WE
we write for free

no one pays for entertainment
outside of sports,
internet and cinematic tv
we are not celebrities

news crews don't sit outside
our houses with curiosity
we are underneath the drown trodden
in polite business society

we are the bane
of the vein's anxiety
outlining the ills
discovered in false piety

we are the few
that would perform our craft

for the peace it brings
we are the original story tellers
for presidents, kings and queens

the artisans at large
the starving freeloader
without a cause
the person people freely tell to get a job

we walk around…
with degrees unused
illustrating scenarios
capable of bursting a brain fuse

meanings get convoluted
wrapped around stories
that truth made bold
in this thriller nickel tales are sold
anything to break through to a jaded soul

Never Hopeless

in the office
at the guard desk
i am the greeter, security and secretary
with a brand ambassador logo on my breast

i'm the first face they see in the lobby
they talk to me like a therapist
give me a few seconds…
gonna burst out in a super woman dress

underneath, this strong persona
is a ton of stress
i spent the last few months,
learning how to make a little money stretch
even though i'm earning less

so i don't end up homeless
at the base of my rigorous, steep mountain
steadily climbing to the top
but i'm still blessed

and capable of surpassing
any endurance test
i cook perseverance up,
serve it and save the rest
leftovers squeezed into a zip-lock,
placed in a freezer chest
makes no difference the situation,
i do my best

my prayers revolve

around building and maintaining
the contents of my soul:

etched from the chalk
of love and happiness
i made a living off
never feeling hopeless

Barbershop Visit

love is on his mind
he gotta look good
office work flow
or chilling in the hood

prayers lie on his shoulders
dreams of fulfilling prophecy
sit in rest around street corners
in close proximity to barbershops

the passion is seen in the angled tilt
of a barber's wrist
carving designs
into an untouched landscape
ready for combing,
pruning and styling bliss

you are the psychologist,
hairdresser and friend
shaving away mist covered memories,
tall tales and shedding distance
relaxation tied into urgent care

easy razors oiled
and pulled across rough patches
few suspect are there
liberally apply alcohol to close edges

grease the epidermis
and the sharp contours

of the hairline
brush away the complicated days
and leave something even in its place

inching closer to progress...
finding that lucid visions await
in the gleaming mirror
presented before your face

a life transformed
by a haircut's saving grace
in this lively station of revised fades
and hairstyling delight
sadness has no place

the passion is seen
in the angled tilt of a barber's wrist
carving designs
into an untouched landscape
ready for combing,
pruning and styling bliss
you are the psychologist,
hairdresser and friend

to clientele with deep pockets
and those barely making ends meet
you have been around
since they were knee high
with hair hanging neck steep

We Live Here

we blow bubbles
as though we occupied a pineapple
at the heart of the sea

we pound words into clay
and use fossilized seaweed
to make cutlery

we are not merpeople
but we live here
a place that defies logic
and misrepresents fear

feet beckoned
by unknown forces draw near
we swim with killer whales
who desire the challenge of going deep
we are entranced by the dolphin's song

it rocks our weary souls to sleep
and with no nightlight
a lighthouse glow is all we need
we inhale the fruit of life via simplicity

We Forgot

we forgot about each other
too busy gossiping bout
sista so and so
while ignoring the plight of our brothers

we push each other to extremes
like we don't know
how brokenness screams

pouring hand squeezed orange juice
into porcelain cups with dirt rings
it tastes delicious
until you realize the container's not clean

we chastise the drug fiend
but visit the pharmacy
forgetting it all started in the same parking lot
how quickly we judge!
how quickly we forgot!

I See The Signs

i see the signal:
the northern lights blinking Morse code
to restless souls
in need of a worthy adventure

the rings are back in play
the power of the elites is switching hands
as the masses clamor
under scrupulous money demands

only to suffer a sleight of hand
at the cost of lost dignity
will you push the coming tide with me?
i see the signs

damned if you do,
damned if you don't guidelines
supervisor told you you're laid off
despite getting sick on the job
and needing to pay medical costs

now you have to carry the expenses
of having no boss
and no severance package
to minimize the loss
the unpaid rent is only enhanced
by the lack of childcare…

who watches the children
when the teachers aren't there?
when their grandparents

are more susceptible
to the Covid-19 in the air?

who do you turn to
when the village can't be there?
trapped in a time
of isolation and great despair

but as the world turns…
i see the signal
the northern lights blinking Morse code
to restless souls
in need of a worthy adventure

How To Hit A Parked Car

back when i was high,
confused by the drive,
refused to take a chance
i let you drive

i watched you,
reverse and ram
into a parked car
in the parking lot
of a rickety old gas station

their front driver side was smashed
crushed it like an empty soda can
i stayed and waited for the cops
you ran.
who does that to a friend?

i let you, rear end
some poor family's Thanksgiving plans
the bungee cord
that held their hood down, gave way

somebody's Momma,
Daddy, Uncle and Aunt
was mad at me/ mad at you/ mad at us
on the south side that day

i bore the heat
you didn't care to feel
the car was liable to me
the damage was real

i stood outside
got my license ready
insurance ready
remarks after a collision ready

but i wasn't prepared
for the sadness
for the shock
for the feelings
wasted on childless youth…
they were the hunger pains i forgot

the gas station owner
stands outside the store looking nonchalant
a headline flashes across my mind:
Student Home For Break
Wrecks Family's Holidays Activities

due to incompetence of the highest kind
to which they responded
you need better people in your life
i was disappointed in myself
and my choices while staring
at lamp post lights

A Glass for Me

pour that there...
bitter wine
let it water
the gathering weeds
aged to perfection,

giving poor directions
to a wispy path
coated by missing sobriety
ignorance runs out into the streets

the broken ground
clamors beneath weighted feet
the sidewalk begs
for something strong
to drink

and once you're done...
tilting the glass
save a little
and pass it to me

Playa With The Cocoa Butter

the *real* searched for by people
like flowers seeking sun
and thirsting for a light shower
but wanting no one

you got that hold up...
"let me put my clothes on"
i'll meet you in an hour
you are the cool side of sunshine
you bring precipitation
to the afternoon shower

i discovered a truthful intricacy
in the prism of your eye
you leave me soft spoken
a shell in a giant ocean

he got the Midas touch
our first kiss was strong
the number 19 love potion
filled my mouth and heart
with endless devotion

your motion is silky
it goes on smooth
like cocoa butter lotion
never too oily or too creamy
just the right consistency

About You

it's the way you laugh...
when you think
no one's listening
the way you groove and move...
to the beat in the shower

the way you get work done
no matter the time of the hour
the way you show up and show out
for your family

the way you balance your daily tasks
it's the curve folded
in the crease of your right arm
it's the light-heartened nature
of your charm
it's the chemistry
of your give and take conversations

it's the civility you display
when you wait and listen for response
it's the fragrant allure of you
that hypnotizes people
as you walk past

well...
to be quite honest,
it's everything about you

Part 2

<u>Heart</u>

For all intents and purposes...
I am true to my heart
The call of it beckons me
And the pain of it
Drives me away
It is the only person
I can't lie to

Sweet Thang

he plotting on a way to unearth my soul
foliage deep rooted in problems
he couldn't console
vines took hold

large tea candles burn in the moonlight
but no conversation emerges
we stare into the orange candescent
coming from a yellow flame
it burns with stalled words and fickle desires

i walk a tightrope on the rim
i remember when i use to love him
bright hearts like clean tiles
in afternoon glow touched
by the hand of bleach
and home sweet home antics

we are here trying to form sand into stone
trying to build up a foundation
we're proud to own
i see you sweet thang

You & Me

old scars heal fast
because you make me laugh
we joke like lost kinfolk
at a barbecue

you bled through
my paper thin resolve
treating my ruptured heart like a jigsaw
you were assigned to solve

whenever i'm over you
i look up to find myself
back underneath you
resuming our ecstasy
heaven is a stone throw away
when you're near me

when you talk to me
even when we argue
we both win
it's just one of the challenges we face
as lovers and best friends

Kryptonite

under the shifting,
rusty lamp lights,
planted in sidewalk cement
moths flutter from left to right,

up and down, out of sight
they intermingle flight routes
and swarm in the warm bliss
of the bulb's luminescence

the night air is inviting…
the breeze takes adventure by the wing
they dream…
to one day get a bit closer to the sun

although the heat may burn their intent
the reckless risk-takers
keep pushing against the inevitable
turning their floating ecstasy
into a sinking fear

they make figure eights
with nautical delight
egging themselves up to get...
just a but closer to their Kryptonite

Flesh's Door

don't know how things got so intense
it's like trust left the room
and took forgiveness with it

we are only feet apart
but the feet feel like miles
we snap at each other like ireful crocodiles
getting testy over a shared meal

your eyes read like braille
the chestnut window frame
with carved initials
taken from my name
encased in a glossy finish
paid witness to your lies

crashing from the inside
onto unforgiving stones
love is all you wanted

but one day
you may come home
to no home

just a washed up fable of bliss
dried out on reality's shore
staring down a cold captivity
but still wanting more

flesh awaits at my door…

It's Just Make Believe

i made it up
the appearance of strength
the wispy laugh, the bashful eyes
the know it all persona

just to get along
fake it till you make it,
served up in a veggie roll
i won't consume
but i expect you to

nonetheless, won't you turn loose with me?
forget about your contempt for me
for just one night
and console all the facades i had to concoct

just to make this turquoise dress fit right...
the mascara that i cried off 4 times today
to arrive here...
and put it on again in the bathroom is a waste
if you don't see it!

all the anthems about independent women
apply to me
until it comes to you...
but i fill my spirit with this lemonade
just in case it gets too hot to handle
and i'm out of shade

caught in a revolving door

of mind numbing brunch, catered lunch
and the occasional masquerade
with little else to do but entertain you
i made it up

Good Men

goodness gracious, have mercy
cover me in your grace
wrap me in your love
turn me not from your face

i have sinned
again and again
dug, deep, dark trenches
for the hearts and souls
of good men

knowing i could never
care for them
i get it in
impaired evenings lavished
with dom pérignon and fast food

at some point
ya gonna speak
only so many times
you can kiss on a man's neck
and make his mind go weak

Wood

it's not love
that petrifies me
it's the thought of losing it

precious feelings slipping through
nimble finger tips
words synthesized in emotions
that lost their grip

we were once a strong oak
with roots immersed with the soil,
tunneling far and wide

branches that held strong
in the breeze,
stretched toward a black sky

never too dark to see
wooden arms stretching
from an aged tree
carved letters outlined in hearts
adorn the Cyprus bark

partners joined at the hip
eclipsed glimpses of sunlight
break up the moonlight stroll

We Drink the Tea

we submerge our notion
of eternity into a steaming kettle
the whistle charges through the house
like a preposterous bull in a rodeo

we strain the vitality of forever
from forest foliage tinted
in shiny emerald splendor

the aroma of tart acidic, loose leaf tea
entices the senses
we inhale paradise...

pour the contents into a stainless saucer
under the veil of an autonomous,
limitless, well-traveled gravel road
we drink nestled in eternity's bosom

Held On To

always carried a lot of stuff
loaded up on your back like a saddle
and let life ride you
slept in fear
and dined in worry

trust no one and love no one
so there is no one to hold on to
cause the obvious won't hurt you
marinade in atrocious news
devour the blues
like a patient in the hospital
fed nutrients through tubes

just don't wanna lose
the last concrete thing
that your heart held on to
it aches for you
beats for you
pray it don't grow weak on you

it is the backbone of the operation
without it no packages can be carried
no barrier can be crossed
no wars can be won
only courage lost

there it is again!
that sound…
it beckons you
clear as a whistle

but you still won't listen
like a cold draft blowing through the window
the soul cries out, "let it go"
if you can't heal, you won't grow

mahogany eyes tell tales deeper than the sea
standing in the present
but reenacting history
hauling the troubles blood ties held on to

refuse to have a child
and pass this curse on to somebody new
break the generational lies
forefathers held on to

always carried a lot of stuff
loaded up on your back like a saddle
and let life ride you
slept in fear
and dined in worry

but those days are gone
when turmoil comes knocking like a flood
from a broken dam, don't open the door
living care free is a rare delicacy
contorted souls can't ignore
new chances are worth creating
change is worth fighting for

the dawn of tomorrow
breathing in the air of today
searching for answers, creating a way
the wise learn from yesterday

Maybe

maybe just maybe
if i can put my hurt into words
i'll be whole again
maybe i can feel something other than
anguish in my soul again
can a sista just be wishful again?

i been trying to rearrange the pieces
like a puzzle i may never solve
i just wanna break people down
the way they tried to break me

bring them to their knees
with fists and misplaced anger
and make them feel unworthy
but does violence in place of violence...
serve me?

i just want to feel as beautiful
as people say i look
they just like the cover
without opening the book
if they knew my story
they wouldn't give me a second look

i want something besides
a uphill battle
i want something besides
fear in my life

i rarely accept hugs
but when i do they make me cringe inside

the sting of punches fade
but the memory of abuse never dies
i love lipstick
it's brilliant cover is my mask
i call it my war paint
every bit of bold

i've been learning the art of makeup
since i was 10 years old
i need a palette
that is spun around gold ambition
a midnight mission

it can tell tales…
when the world refuses to listen
yeah, that's what this smudged eyeliner is all about
it's the tears that my parents, siblings and ex-lovers
ignored

i have a hate and love relationship with pretty
it ain't never protected me from harm
but if anyone calls me anything other than that
it sets off alarms

can someone hold me...
from a distance?
i cry on their shoulder from a far
and they stand there and listen

a shelter dog, black as onyx saved me

we both dealing with PTSD
i was knee deep in myself sabotage
when he helped me

when i come home he cries
when i leave he cries
he never expects me to come back
but I do

anyone that's been left out in the cold
understands what he's going through
sometimes, I look at him
and think who has more issues?
maybe if i recover he will too

Pursuit Of A Breaking Dream

why live if you never learn?
don't jump into pill and coke lines
proud to take a dangerous turn
shorty blowing dust
like she got an urn

we beefing over cash, grass and a man
with his eyes fixed
on everybody ass
you racing but getting nowhere fast
cause you're out of gas

weeping willows cry for thee
mourning over a future
our ancestors bleed for
but were unable to see

a people torn from Africa
searching from sea to shining sea
for a place to exist
for a home that's truly free
where we don't have to worry
about glass ceilings breaking our dreams

Exist

don't smash me into your
picture perfect, modish suburban family of four
affirmed Kodak frame staples
offset by social media acclaim

i learned a long time ago...
that my lavish thighs were too wide for lenses
they can't be boxed into geometric spheres
they can't be tamed, Lord knows i tried...
but they exist still...

the golden ratio fails to capture
the delicate swoops of my full lips
it is predicated against
the vibrant flare of my nostrils
it cares nothing for the creases
at the corner of my slanted eyes
but they exist still...

whether by fate or my will
i will love this canvas of mine
cradled and protected
by turned up lashes,

buried in the center
of a black pupil is unrefined glory
waiting to be unsealed
to a world full of fictitious stories
to prove they exist still...

Colorblind

this year
i repeat, this year
has been a complete mess
yes, i'm blessed

but i'm over the constraints i detest
covid-19, self-isolation, enduring racism and civil
unrest
put boulders on a heavy chest
but I'm still standing
with all the strength God gave me

i'm more focused than angry
but even if i was...
who could blame me?
i'm tired of being sick and tired

it doesn't matter how smart you are
if your life is hanging by a wire
a hollow thought for real freedom
awakened by tear filled protests and riot fire

i continue to thrive through my oppression...
why continue to hate me?
create near impossible scenarios
for Black people then say we're lying

cover the sordid reality with criminalizing fables
many are capable but few are able
as though the system ain't built
to abuse and or kill non-whites

if they cross an invisible red line
the elites keep moving the goal post
but expect the Black people of the globe
to keep acting like everything's fine

while poverty is at an all-time high
families are losing their houses and livelihoods
quicker than someone popping the cork off a bottle
of wine
the government is stalling
by buying used time

hiding...
from everyday people's imposed turmoil
wishing...
they turn to a life of crime
how can justice be just
while hired politicians play colorblind?

and that's why
i'm more focused than angry
but even if i was...
who could blame me?
i'm tired of being sick and tired

Part 3

Hope

Love is the incubator of all seeds...
Give patience and water to your dreams
Never underestimate the creek
Where hope springs

God's Security

beneath the masses concentrated on dwindling
savings
are voices of inadequacy
have i failed myself?
how will i take care of my family?
what will happen to me?

can i afford to work?
if uncle sam opens work?
when the cost may be impending gloom...
labored breath,
and no relatives in the waiting room

the odious wait inside this box
gnaws at security
cries in solitude
landing on bended knee
to pray for inner peace:

bush set ablaze by God's voice
speak to me
speak to me

still water clam under foot
usher me forward
usher me forward

let a few loaves be broken
to feed the masses
let the ocean's catch
give fuel to the multitude

nourish my spirit Oh Lord
light a hope inside of me
to dispel the darkness
so the blind can see

make my path even
supply my overhead
supplement my income with faith

i reached out to local politicians
only to receive no answer
if the world is the body
then Covid's creation is the cancer

bush set ablaze by God's voice
speak to me
speak to me

still water clam under foot
usher me forward
usher me forward

The Way It Is

we are two halves
of the same whole
striving to complete ourselves
without each other

arguing like lion cubs
with the same mother
that's what you are to me
the other side of the pillow close

it's hard to get rid of you
you are a parasite
and I'm the host
but you're still my best friend
whom i trust the most
and that's the way it is

I wrote this poem about my Sister aka my best friend. Sometimes I miss home and poetry always takes me back there.

You Are the Heartbeat

creation was organic
love fell into specified slots
like the stars alignment
hopes, fears, goals and ancestral stories
folded into a newborn's skin,
tempted with parental love

you are the heartbeat
they never knew they needed
the blessing that keeps on giving
you are the fresh green seedling
they nursed into a plant
water alone wasn't enough

so they encouraged you to take in the sun
stationary life wouldn't suit you
so they encouraged you to run
explore, get up and fall down
so you know how to overcome

mother so short and sweet
father so tall and kind
big brother lost to the concrete
little sister is like my shadow

always watching, never far behind but rarely
speaks
is she mute? people ask me

no, she is mindful
and always discrete
much like me…

you are the heartbeat
they never knew they needed
the blessing that keeps on giving
you are the fresh green seedling
they nursed into a plant

one day,
you will start your own garden
but when you leave know
there is a home that wants you back

in the kitchen cultivated by housewife dreams
our mother is on standby
in a nightgown, hair bonnet and slippers
with an open fire on the stove

she smiles softly from her brown barely open eyes
and says, *how many eggs do you want baby?*
i missed you when you were away
no matter how long you are gone…
your mother always waits

This poem is dedicated to my wonderful Father.

Fishing For Catch

on quite mornings,
before dusk had a chance
to break the sky
before the morning
dew illuminates flower petals
my father would take me
to the river bank

to relive/ relieve/ recreate and return
to the land of his memory bank
where grandfather taught him
the power of casting a reel
and sitting still

this is how, we put food on the table
this is how, we foot the bill
passed down through generations
fresh fish by the scale
no need for groceries
catfish without retail

Dad says,
nice and easy, calm and smooth
the fish can feel, your every move
they are in tune, with the vibration
don't let excitement, rise, unnecessary anticipation
the end of the line, is nothing, to play with

so we read and sit
we inch steady
only grabbing, the pole, with speed
when ready
my dad likes the peace

i developed allergies
so he no longer brings me
but the bank
has the same allure still…
you lose, not for a lack of strength
but for a lack of skill

on quite mornings,
before dusk had a chance
to break the sky
before the morning
dew illuminates flower petals
my father would take me
to the river bank

The Root

i hope peace will meet you
where blue eyed love
failed to entreat you
i pray for your healed liver
and renewed soul

a shoulder to lean on,
a cheek to hold
an ear to revive story,
a smile to greet you
and a mouth to utter praise

a safety to protect you
the rest of your spiritual days
a decagon stands between you
and I but i miss you still

we call you the matriarch
your onions and potatoes
brought everyone home at night
just to get a taste of your food
the children started acting right

you are the glue
the cornerstone of our family
that southern Mississippi blues
and funk gave birth to

you are the future and the past
the influence we look to
when our strength won't last

you are the Root!

i hope peace will meet you
where blue eyed love
failed to entreat you

i pray for your healed liver
and renewed soul
a shoulder to lean on,
a cheek to hold

Just Stubborn

this is me
wearing my fever
the things that time, won't heal
or is it my will?

i won't let go
the heart says, *i'm exhausted*
but the mind says, *no*
never fold

this is me
feeling unimpressed with myself
running from the truth
and wishing to be someone else
but yet and still
trying to love myself

this is me
being mad at my boyfriend
because i'm mad at myself
telling him i wouldn't care if he leaves
but knowing deep down inside
i don't want nobody else

i pray he don't let go
the heart says, *i'm exhausted*
but the mind says, *no*
never fold

this is me
avoiding the gym

because i don't like to be sore
the suns' out, i'm feeling good
what do i need to work out for

until i looked in the mirror
and saw a muffin top
i couldn't ignore
now i'm back in the gym
wondering what I stopped for?

this is me
working on my career
overcoming my stage fright
and working through my ever mounting fears
because, I can't let go
the heart says, *i'm exhausted*
but the mind says, *no*
never fold
this is me

This Here

this here room, got good to me
these walls, know…
the inner workings of me
they put me to ease

lean on em,
pound on em,
fuck on em,
cry on them
ask the Lord, *why on them?*

knowing…
they would never respond to me
my goodness,
if they had the power of speech
i envy their secrecy

seen me,
throw on the facade
that dispelled the face of truth

seen me,
dress
and undress
only to redress my weight

seen me,
pray for forgiveness
at man's gate
only to a bare a dire faith

this here room,
got good to me
these walls, know…
the inner workings of me
they put me to ease

lean on em,
pound on em,
fuck on em,
cry on them
ask the Lord, *why on them?*

they are the base that holds me up
the friends offering my soul
the quiet advice it needs
forming solid barriers around me
preparing me for the world
when i'm not ready

Battle Cry

you struggle,
i struggle,
we struggle
because we're family

it hurts me
to see you trying
so desperately

don't hide the anguish
you feel inside
let the world hear
your battle cry

Ambition

today we glide with sparrows
and tonight we join owls
in their merrymaking
no need to use man's door

our ambitions span the expansive sky
greeting helicopters like passersby
then in the midnight hour
we ride the moon's tide

we are travelers
carrying suitcases on hills
created by our own feet
when we go low
we get bottom of the ocean deep

we are dreams in progress
resting on a stalled breath
we are the story born
when the world seeks to reset

we watched the hands
of father time sire wane and wonder
we have no respect for titles
that change owners like leaves in the wind

What is Freedom?

is it the substance
of things unseen?
like the chime
of a cell phone ring?

or is it…
the storm's silver lining
the feeling of coasting
in a far off island

the feeling of being
with a down ass brotha
and you stand beside him
when the dropping weather
is uninviting?

or is it…
like propaganda and lies
being sold to the youth
the chill of icy sentiments
rubbing against the truth

it's the clean smell of soap
and warm laundry dried
it's in the tap of the heel
and the rhythm's feel,
combined into one...

the reason God gave
his only begotten son
which brings us back
to the question of freedom

Be Easy

do not retreat
when the rain comes
eyeliner gallops
it don't run

be easy
like a small river
winding over crescent hills

be patience
after the whirlwind,
nature goes still

be smooth
like a pimple
that's been covered with toothpaste

be flexible
like air
life takes many shapes

be steady
like lovers that mature
most bottles, go stale, fine wine endures

be loud
like a squeaky wheel
break up, the silence, you feel

be abrasive
like sandpaper to skin
be felt, without the need, to fit in

be brazen
like a cheater with no shame
smudged truth hidden under eraser stains

do not retreat
when the rain comes
eyeliner gallops
it don't run

Self-Discovery

there's this point,
when your back is to the wall
and you have nowhere to run
nowhere left to hide

nowhere to look but inside
but in this moment,
when it seems like
all is lost

and the walls are caving in
you will discover
what it truly means
to be alive

What is Friendship?

There was a time when friendship amounted to more than heads nodding in agreement and a round of applause for achievements. It was a base to keep you honest and humble.

They are the people that tell you the truth and hold you to it even when it hurts them to do so. They inform you of your wrong doing even if it could cost them everything!

To be a true friend at times you must sacrifice the comfortable conversations for the uncomfortable ones. It is in those moments that we find growth that far exceeds the pleasure of stroking our egos.

It is in those moments that we are able to define *true friendship*. On our good and bad days on a pedestal made of wood and clay or laying on an unforgiving floor we find the essence of relationships and it is in this bevy of uncertainty in my life that I find you.

No matter where today leads you, remember that you are loved and that you are love. Thank you for being a friend.

Forever yours, Esha

www.ingramcontent.com/pod-product-compliance
Lightning Source LLC
Chambersburg PA
CBHW030154070426
42447CB00032B/1197